ANIMAL ALLIES

POLAR BEARS AND ARCTIC FOXES
TEAM UP!

BY STEPHANIE PETERS

CAPSTONE PRESS
a capstone imprint

Published by Capstone Press, an imprint of Capstone.
1710 Roe Crest Drive, North Mankato, Minnesota 56003
capstonepub.com

Library of Congress Cataloging-in-Publication Data
Names: Peters, Stephanie True, 1965- author.
Title: Polar bears and arctic foxes team up! / by Stephanie Peters.
Description: North Mankato, Minnesota : Capstone Press, an imprint of Capstone, [2023] | Series: Animal allies | Includes bibliographical references and index. | Audience: Ages 8 to 11 | Audience: Grades 4-6 | Summary: " Polar bears and arctic foxes team up for a hunt in this photo-filled nonfiction book for young research writers and wildlife fans. One powerful polar bear + one sly arctic fox = a dream team! Discover how two vastly different animal species team up to find food. With super-smell and tremendous strength, polar bears are the Arctic's deadliest hunters. So much so, these big-time beasts often have leftovers. Cue the arctic foxes! These clever opportunists are game for any game and will clean up after polar bears, lickety-split. With eye-popping photographs, quick facts, and beyond-the-book back matter, Polar Bears and Arctic Foxes Team Up ! will have young research writers and wildlife fans rooting for these Animal Allies"-- Provided by publisher.
Identifiers: LCCN 2022052693 (print) | LCCN 2022052694 (ebook) | ISBN 9781669048800 (hardcover) | ISBN 9781669048756 (paperback) | ISBN 9781669048763 (ebook PDF) | ISBN 9781669048787 (kindle edition) | ISBN 9781669048794 (epub)
Subjects: LCSH: Polar bear--Behavior--Juvenile literature. | Arctic fox--Behavior--Juvenile literature. | Mutualism (Biology)--Juvenile literature.
Classification: LCC QL737.C27 P424 2023 (print) | LCC QL737.C27 (ebook) | DDC 599.776/4--dc23/eng/20230126
LC record available at https://lccn.loc.gov/2022052693
LC ebook record available at https://lccn.loc.gov/2022052694

Editorial Credits
Editor: Donald Lemke; Designer: Sarah Bennett; Media Researcher: Svetlana Zhurkin; Production Specialist: Katy LaVigne

Image Credits
Alamy: Imagebroker, 17; Dreamstime: Anthony Hathaway, 5, Erectus, 13; Getty Images: Darrell Gulin, 23, Design Pics/Robert Postma, cover (top left), Gabrielle Therin-Weise, 22, milehightraveler, 15, Paul Souders, 9, 27, robertharding/Thorsten Milse, 4; Newscom: Danita Delimont Photography/Steve Kazlowski, 16; Shutterstock: Alexey Seafarer, cover (top right), 11, 28, 29, Danita Delimont, 18, FloridaStock, 14, Goinyk Production, cover (bottom), GTW, 24, Heiko Wittenborn, 12, NeoLeo (background), cover (top middle) and throughout, nwdph, 6, polarman, 8, rooh183, 19, Tony Campbell, 7, Vlad G, 10, Yuliya Chsherbakova (background), cover (bottom), back cover, and throughout; Superstock: Minden Pictures/ Michio Hoshino, 20–21, Photoshot/NHPA, 25

Printed and bound in the USA. 5425

Table of Contents

Words in **bold** are in the glossary.

CHAPTER ONE

The Need to Feed

It's a late spring morning in coastal Alaska. All is quiet and still. Then a black nose pokes out of a snowbank. The nose is attached to a skinny female polar bear. She emerges from her den for the first time in weeks. Her two young cubs follow closely behind.

A polar bear mother with cubs

ringed seal

The mother bear hasn't eaten all winter. She plods onto the sea ice. She sniffs the air, trying to catch the scent of **prey**. Her eyes scan left to right. Her ears twitch. Suddenly, she stops.

In the distance near the water's edge lies a sleek ringed seal. The mother bear signals to her cubs with a low, *chuff-chuff* sound. They halt in their tracks.

A mile away, a lone arctic fox trots on the rocky hillside. He's searching for food when a light breeze carries a familiar scent to his nostrils. It's the smell of a nearby polar bear. Usually, he would steer clear of the much bigger **predator**. But not this time.

Following his nose, the arctic fox picks his way down the rocks to the snow-covered **tundra** below. Then he hurries toward the coast—and the polar bear family.

Meanwhile, the mother bear flattens her body against the ice and tucks her front paws underneath her. Then, using her powerful hind legs, she slowly pushes herself toward the seal. Snow mounds up in front of her black nose as she edges closer and closer.

The ringed seal suns himself, completely unaware that he is being stalked.

But the mother bear doesn't attack—not yet. Instead, she slips silently into the water. The cubs straighten. They've never tasted meat before, only their mother's milk. They've never hunted before, either. This is their first lesson.

The arctic fox also watches. Like the mother polar bear, he is very hungry. If she catches the seal, he might fill his belly too.

DID YOU KNOW?

Female polar bears can go without food for more than 180 days before they need to eat.

CHAPTER TWO

Cold Climate Companions

Polar bears are the largest four-legged **carnivores** on Earth. They are uniquely adapted to survive in their frozen environment. Like snowshoes, their wide, flat feet keep them from sinking into deep snow. Their sharp claws grip the ice. Long, powerful back legs make them fast runners.

Polar bears are also excellent swimmers. They do the dog-paddle, their huge feet propelling them forward after prey. Their flat, triangular heads help them knife through the surf. Their nostrils close when they're underwater.

Two layers of thick, waterproof fur keep polar bears warm in frigid temperatures in and out of the water. That fur looks white, but it's actually made of clear, hollow shafts that turn white when light hits them. White fur is the perfect **camouflage** in the snow and helps the polar bear sneak up on its prey.

DID YOU KNOW?

The polar bear is also known as the sea bear because of its swimming ability.

Arctic foxes are small, nimble **omnivores**. Like polar bears, they've adapted to living in below-freezing temperatures. They have furry footpads to protect their feet from the frozen tundra. Small ears, short legs, and short muzzles mean they lose less body heat. Many layers of fur help keep their bodies warm too.

Unlike polar bears whose fur stays white year-round, arctic foxes change color depending on the season. In the winter, their fur is bright white to help them camouflage in the snow.

An arctic fox in winter

Arctic fox fur turns darker in warmer seasons.

In the spring and summer, that white fur turns darker. When there's little or no snow, their fur is shades of gray and brown to help them blend in with the rocks and ground around them. In the fall, the dark fur molts and new white fur grows in. Then the cycle begins again.

Besides their white coloring, polar bears and arctic foxes share one other trait: an amazing sense of smell. A polar bear can smell a seal half a mile away. If the seal is swimming just below the snow and ice, the bear can smell it there too!

An arctic fox can detect the scent of its favorite prey, lemmings, in their burrows under the ground and beneath the snow. They can even smell frozen lemmings trapped in ice!

Arctic foxes can also detect a seal **carcass** left by a polar bear from more than 20 miles (30 kilometers) away. Researchers believe that the foxes track the bears themselves by their scent, and then follow that scent in the hopes of feasting on the bear's leftovers.

CHAPTER THREE

A One-Sided Relationship

Polar bears are known as **apex hunters**. That means no other animal hunts them for food. Arctic foxes, on the other hand, can become prey to other predators. Wolverines, wolves, golden eagles, and snowy owls will all hunt and kill arctic foxes for food. Polar bears will too, if they're hungry enough.

A polar bear chases an arctic fox in Alaska.

A polar bear feeds on a carcass with an arctic fox nearby.

So why would an arctic fox risk going anywhere near a polar bear? The answer is food.

DID YOU KNOW?

Other apex predators include lions, tigers, orcas, and saltwater crocodiles.

An arctic fox holds a duck egg in its teeth.

Arctic foxes are opportunist hunters. That means they'll eat just about anything they can catch or find. Usually, they eat rodents, birds, eggs, insects, reptiles, and other small prey they can kill on their own.

DID YOU KNOW?

When an arctic fox hears a lemming beneath the snow, it jumps high in the air, lands hard enough to break through the snow, and snatches its meal with its teeth.

But in winter and early spring, those food sources can be scarce. That's when the hungry arctic fox seeks out the polar bear and the scraps of food the bear leaves behind after feasting on a kill.

The polar bear and arctic fox have a **symbiotic** relationship. That's when two different animal species have a close connection. Sometimes, both animals benefit from their connection. That's called **mutualism**. Sometimes, one animal benefits, but the other is harmed. That's called **parasitism**. Sometimes, only one animal benefits; the other doesn't benefit, but it isn't harmed, either. That's called **commensalism**.

Polar bears and arctic foxes have a commensal relationship. The polar bear doesn't get anything from the fox, but it doesn't lose anything, either. The fox, on the other hand, gets a meal after the polar bear makes a kill.

CHAPTER FOUR

Full Bellies . . . for Now

Back on the coastal ice, the ringed seal stretches and yawns in the sunlight. Suddenly, mother polar bear explodes up through the water. She surges onto the ice and lunges for the seal. The seal tries to dive to safety. But the bear is too fast. She sinks her teeth into his neck and drags him away from the water's edge. The seal is no match for her powerful jaws.

A polar bear drags its prey across the ice.

At their mother's signal, the cubs join her to feed. They use their sharp teeth to rip and chew the seal blubber. When they all have had their fill, they amble back toward their snowbank den. Only then does the arctic fox make his way to the kill.

An arctic fox feeds on the leftovers of a seal carcass.

The fox devours as much as his stomach will hold. Then he buries scraps here and there in the snow. He'll dig up these hidden snacks in the winter when food is scarce. Finally, he carries a few morsels to his underground burrow. Yipping happily, his mate and their pups dine on the tasty treats.

The polar bear and arctic fox families all have full bellies this day. But they might not be so lucky in the future.

CHAPTER FIVE

Climate Challenges

Polar bears and arctic foxes are dependent on their snowy, icy environment for food. But **climate change**, which causes ocean temperatures to rise, is melting the sea ice and shrinking the tundra. And animals like the arctic fox and polar bear are paying the price.

More water and less land mean fewer lemmings, the arctic fox's primary food source. The scraps from polar bear kills aren't enough to keep them fed. When foxes go hungry, they have fewer pups or no litters at all. Any pups that are born go hungry . . . or starve to death.

DID YOU KNOW?

In the early 1900s, arctic foxes were killed by the thousands for their beautiful white fur. Nowadays, such hunting is strictly controlled.

Polar bears are suffering greatly too. They live, hunt, and give birth on sea ice and ice floes. As the sea ice melts, their hunting grounds shrink and move farther apart. These expert swimmers struggle to cover the distances between floes. Some don't make it.

If climate change continues to harm their environment, these mighty predators might lose their battle for survival.

POLAR BEAR

Also Known As: Sea bear

Species: *Ursus maritimus*—family includes black, brown, and grizzly bears

Size: 4–4.5 feet (1.2–1.4 meters) tall at shoulder; 7–8 feet (2.1–2.4 m) long from nose to tail

Weight: 600–800 pounds (272–363 kilograms) for females; 1,000–1,600 pounds (454–726 kg) for males

Fur: Coarse, transparent shafts that look white in light

Features: Powerful jaws; triangular, flat head; wide feet with sharp claws; black nose and eyes, black skin

As a Hunting Ally: Leaves behind seal remains for arctic fox to scavenge.

ARCTIC FOX

Also Known As: Polar fox, snow fox, white fox

Species: *Vulpes lagopus*—family includes red foxes

Size: 20–30 inches (51–76 centimeters) long from nose to tail

Weight: 6.5–7.5 pounds (2.9–3.4 kg)

Fur: Thick with multiple layers, changes from brown and gray in summer to pure white in winter

Features: Small ears; short legs; short muzzles; large, fluffy tail; brown, yellow, blue, or bicolored eyes

As a Hunting Ally: Benefits from the polar bear's kill.

Glossary

apex hunter (AY-peks HUN-ter)—a top predator that is not hunted by other animals

camouflage (KAM-oh-flazh)—an animal's natural coloring or shape that lets it blend in with its surroundings

carcass (KAR-kuhs)—the body of a dead animal

carnivore (KAR-nuh-vor)—an animal that feeds on flesh

climate change (CLI-muht CHANJ)—a change in the globe's ocean temperatures and weather patterns

commensalism (koh-MEN-sul-izm)—a relationship where one animal benefits and the other is unharmed

mutualism (MYOO-choo-uhl-ism)—a partnership that benefits both animals

omnivore (AHM-nuh-vor)—an animal that feeds on both meat and plants

parasitism (PEHR-uh-sit-izm)—a relationship where one animal benefits and another is harmed

predator (PRED-i-tor)—an animal that naturally preys on other animals

prey (PRAY)—an animal that is hunted and killed by other animals, usually for food

symbiotic (sim-by-OT-ik)—a close relationship and interaction between two animal species

tundra (TUN-druh)—a flat region of ice and snow with no trees

Read More

Farley, Christin. *The Little Book of Animals of the Arctic.* Fresno, CA: Bushel & Peck, 2022.

Janes, Patricia. *Arctic Foxes.* New York: Scholastic, 2019.

Viola, Jason. *Science Comics: Polar Bears: Survival on the Ice.* New York: First Second, 2018.

Internet Sites

National Geographic: Arctic Fox
nationalgeographic.com/animals/mammals/facts/arctic-fox

World Wildlife Foundation: Arctic Fox
https://www.worldwildlife.org/species/arctic-fox

World Wildlife Foundation: Polar Bear
worldwildlife.org/species/polar-bear

Index

About the Author

Stephanie Peters has been writing books for young readers for more than 25 years. Among her most recent titles are *Sleeping Beauty: Magic Master* and *Johnny Slimeseed*, both for Capstone's Far-Out Fairy Tales and Folk Tales series. An avid reader, workout enthusiast, and beach wanderer, Stephanie enjoys spending time with her children, Jackson and Chloe, her husband Dan, and the family's two cats and two rabbits. She lives and works in Mansfield, Massachusetts.